WORLD WITHOUT END

DEL SNELLER

Hi Kathy --
Thanks for your friendship, especially during these hard days.
Del + Jereen
9-1-11

To my wife, Jereen.

WORLD WITHOUT END

DEL SNELLER

American Literary Press, Inc.
Five Star Special Edition
Baltimore, Maryland

WORLD WITHOUT END

Copyright © 1996 Del Sneller

All rights reserved under International and Pan-American copyright conventions. No part of this book may be reproduced, stored in a retrieval system, or transmitted in any form, electronic, mechanical, or other means, now known or hereafter invented, without written permission of the publisher. Address all inquiries to the publisher.

Grateful acknowledgement is made to the following journals in which some of the poems first appeared: *Stone Country, Bardic Echoes, Quill Books, United Methodist Reporter, Quaker Life, Garfield Lake Review, Seems, Huerfano, Hope College Opus, Night Roses, Moose Bound Press, The White Crow.*

"Thursday's Girl," "Watching Leslie Anne's Birth," "To R. About Beetles," and "Deathling" are reprinted with permission from *The Place in the Woods/Read America!*

Library of Congress
Cataloging in Publication Data
ISBN 1-56167-321-8

Library of Congress Card Catalog Number: 96-069569

Published by

American Literary Press, Inc.
Five Star Special Edition
8019 Belair Road, Suite 10
Baltimore, Maryland 21236

Manufactured in the United States of America

CONTENTS

IF THERE WERE NOTHING

2	Ice Fishing
3	Drummond Island
4	Alcoholic
5	Old Times
6	Accident on 64th Street
7	Into Darkness I Will Work
8	The Third Cross
9	Country Schoolhouse
10	Thursday's Girl
11	Church
12	Tornado
13	Deathling
14	Ice Storm
15	Alzheimer's
16	Sentence
17	Great Grandmother

SPEECH POURING DOWN

20	Old Mission Point
21	Star Saffire
22	At Her Time of Death
23	Visiting Her House
24	The Mongoloid and the Luna
25	Late Derecho
26	Last Night

27	Solitary Definement
28	My Wife
29	Document
30	Reverie
31	Trappist
32	Abide with Me
33	Passing Confession
34	Epitaph for a Strict Lady
35	Afterword
36	Stormy Communion
37	Mill
38	Emily Dickinson
39	Blackberries

DO NOT BE AFRAID

42	Uterinus
43	Mary
44	Straw
45	Jesus and the Prostitute
46	Peter
49	Lazarus
50	Law
51	Joseph of Arimathea
52	Easter
53	Gift
54	For Love Is Strong as Death
55	Holy Spirit
56	Angels
57	To Missing Persons
58	Punish Not My Rest
59	Another Sky

60	Wanderer's Meditation
61	Saint Joseph's Academy
62	October 13, 1917
63	The Reverend Timothy Brown
64	Father, Forgive Them

CATCH THE WINDS

66	Ted Banta
67	Manny Sandoval
68	Watching Leslie Anne's Birth
69	To R. About Beetles
70	Green the Lilac Wood
71	And End
72	Sandy
73	Early Snow
74	Fenn Valley Vineyards
77	Selah
78	Saint Teresa of Avila
79	Shall We Discuss I Love You
81	Under the Tremendous Oak
83	Sing of This
84	Prophet
85	More than Ever
86	Bluebird Coops
87	Beech Trees

IF THERE WERE NOTHING

Experience, it is said, makes a man wise. This is very silly talk. If there were nothing beyond experience, it would simply drive him mad.

Kierkegaard

ICE FISHING

Remember our loss
For words when the spud
Fractured bright ice
And we saw water under us
Dark as any night?

Nothing alive touched our line
All day. Wind pressed water
Towards our feet, and trees,
Simplified to print, warned
How slowly sun-addicted woods
Go dormant under snow.

At last we walked home
Across the lake
While night soaked
Upward past the stars.

Everything must have its say;
The darkness under midday ice
No less than wolf-throat sky.

DRUMMOND ISLAND

A penny and a bowl of violets –
Just these for sunset in December skies
And snow that falls in endless alphabets.
What meanings drift about, who can surmise?
The old folks living in these woods agree
All life gets buried in the sky. A deer,
Albino, shot and chained against a tree,
A trophy (whose, no one remembers here)
Stands guard along our road. I sometimes see
Its eyes glare pink when car lights turn the bend.
This broken unicorn, this mystery,
Has kept the hunters from our woods. The wind

Preserves the form of someone's fear unknown
And pities those who walk this road alone.

ALCOHOLIC

Sorrow beat his hands thin –
Transparent.
His life hung
Crooked on the wall.

He understood the wasp stinging itself
The hexagon of pain
The large rooms
He swept with his heart.

He tumbled away from us
Slowly like a kite –
The broken string
Just out of reach.

OLD TIMES

Grandpa carries winter
Up the basement stairs
Wrapped in a black blanket.

God whispers, "abandoned pear trees" –
A place where nothing works
And choice protects no dream.
The hunter in the useless snow

Sorts rest from rest
And home from home.
A deepening upward goes

And frightened crows
Must try the sky again.
Noise quick as thought
Scatters rose hips on the ice.

ACCIDENT ON 64TH STREET

The police thought she was a child
Standing in the tall grass –
Her legs gone, where the guard rail cut.
She twirled her arms and was carried away.

Love and logic failed.
Even the priest's wild card got lost.
Black ice took her – torn
Like the dust jacket of a book.

INTO DARKNESS I WILL WORK

He packs fire into his Rob Roy pipe.
"Yes, you are the one
Just the one
To clear this field."

I wonder why this bee farmer
His Amish beard white as clover
Why he wants the stones
Rolled from his field of hives.

The sun pulls day – pulls with me
All the stones into the woods.
I shovel under heavy stones; it is good
To reach into the earth, a firmer hold.

But I should leave this place
For daylight closes cold.
Still awake, the field shouts
"Work!" Earth's way of laughing.

His beard nods across the field;
He brings a cup of honey wine.
There was no winter thaw to let
The bees go out. Almost all have died.

Tomorrow plow. I will help.

THE THIRD CROSS

I am an angry man
Too dangerous to taste old wine;
An angry man
Hurried to death by the guessing rain.

I am left alone;
"The King" takes all the blame.
Like the temple I fall apart
Just the distance of a voice from God.

A broken thought pockets
The quiet clock of the sun.
God's kept animals fear
What is real but not true.

Like a heron I bend to sleep
Against the burlap mask of the moon.

COUNTRY SCHOOLHOUSE

I remember wood donated
For winter burning; painted
Barn boards, posts marbled with mold
And soft limbs dropped by storms.

And I remember how the classroom
Looked like a cemetery –
All the desk tops up,
Everyone reaching for a book.

Ice locked swing chains in the yard
While inside all our questions
Steamed the windowpanes.
I listened to everything

The wet wood said to fire.

THURSDAY'S GIRL

How shall I forgive my tenth year
Under that winter blue sun
When my brother's touch made blood
And pain broke the hollow school?

Behind my eyes, every night,
I cried; the Bible
Unlocked my bedroom door.
Hell fits a child's heart.

Around our begged Christmas
Tree, father gave heavy kisses.
In her hand filthy mother
Held Bethlehem's star like a slap.

They kept me in the attic
Above that shameless house.
While snow sifted through the walls,
Bedbugs ate my innocence.

C - The Place In The Woods/Read, America! 1996
Reprinted with permission

CHURCH

Let belief fly
Like leaves across woods.
No more burning
With prayer's single match.

And put the bread and wine
Outside. The birds
Will find the bread
And rain will wash the cup.

For church
Find work begun
But not yet finished.
Storm-wrecked maples wait

Like crosses to be taken down.

TORNADO

Only a killdeer broke
The silence of ambush,
The silence of wrong sky.
Everything turned whiskey yellow.

Wind's glass plow
Worked fields, fast and strange.
Trees bumped heads
Under enormous carousels of cloud.

Then wind stood on end;
A gray stick beat the earth
Toward us. I felt the town
Move over. Little remained: breath

Against thin winter rain,
Broken ribs of hills,
All hunger for settlement – scattered.
I remember ponds that vanished

With backs of mirrors
And a stallion
Left standing,
Killed by a clock.

DEATHLING

She will leave her heart
Outside for many years
Who lost her babe
Before his birth.

The nurse picked him up
Like a broken toy.
She still listens for his name –
An off-hand remark lost between rooms.

She reaches for him, somewhere
Farther than her thoughts can go.
She lives in Rainy Day.
I should hold her

While she reads this.
A friend should do that.

C- The Place In The Woods/Read, America! 1996
Reprinted with permission

ICE STORM

A neighbor's window rises –
The only star.

Hidden, the moon pulls
The ticking tide of the storm.

Junipers bow east
Above the shine of undecided roads.

White oaks know the art of playing dead;
Hands folded over buds.

And the jar of moss stays green
Along the albino path.

The storm stops our clocks;
Twice we set them close to right.

But the one in the barn we leave
Wrong. There ice and steel bang –

A lonely place gone insane
With the noise of time thrown away.

ALZHEIMER'S

Last night icicles let their lightning out
And morning nailed the sun to earth.

Far from the door
He folds the snow like a flag.
Daffodils, before they bloom,
Are flowers still to touch
Beneath the shallow sky of ice.

His days are shadows gone too deep to cast;
His dreams all wither in his sleep.

SENTENCE

There are always words
Without a place to go –
Words drifting quietly as smoke
Level with the winter woods.

There are always words
Too far away to hold –
Far as the heron's flight
Lost to sight against March sun.

There are always words
Deserving shape and sound –
Words lost inside
Haunting thought like time.

There are always words
But only these I give to you:
It doesn't matter anymore
What you've done to me.

GREAT GRANDMOTHER

I

With a red bandanna
Around her head
She leaned forward
And read the Dutch Bible
To her blue parakeet.

> Like a pirate
> Tracing ways to gold
> She leaned forward.

II

Balanced against a wooden golf club
Turned upside down
She led her blind friend
Between rows of poppies
To the porch.

> Kittens, eyes just opened,
> Patted low lilac leaves.

III

While winds warm as pheasant blood
Scattered October
Against evening rooms of blue curtains,

> She reached into her shadow
> And was seen no more.

IV

In her house years later
Among violets and delft saucers
I emptied a jar.

        Embalmed in cinnamon,
        Her blue parakeet
        Dropped into my hands.

SPEECH POURING DOWN

The rain surrounded the whole cabin with its enormous virginal myth, a whole world of meaning, of secrecy, of silence, of rumor. Think of it: all that speech pouring down... Nobody started it, nobody is going to stop it. It will talk as long as it wants, this rain. As long as it talks I am going to listen.

                                            Thomas Merton

OLD MISSION POINT

Think of this
As the beginning of a conversation.
Is poetry ever more than this?

The white-lined sphinx
Says something
Above your rock gardens.
Do you hear
How the willows want for rain?

And the quick, cold wind shift
Across Grand Traverse Bay
And the blue-lined snake
Under the myrtle – these research
Our worry and loneliness.

Wouldn't it be something
If all our years together
Are talking behind our backs
Mentioning the only name
All our thoughts long to say?

Wouldn't it be something
If we must be silent to be heard
And God will kiss us when we come home?

       to C. David and Lillian Mead

STAR SAFFIRE

The Depression did not stop the snow
And the snow did not stop her.

First we heard the clanking of her milk bottles
Hauled five miles from her farm
Twice a week to grandma's house –
A wooden sled of small, harsh bells
Chasing cardinals into the chinkapin.

Then we saw her red kerchief
And black wool coat
And the wide, white apron she always wore.
Seventy years old, she was as round
And strong as the hills she crossed.

While grandma had her in for coffee,
Grandpa worked downstairs; the milk lady
Could not abide his cigars.
I asked her once, when sunrise caught her face –
Why her right eye held a cross of light.

She said, when light enters blindness,
It always makes a cross.

AT HER TIME OF DEATH

I

I grieve at the blue well of day;
The sun is such a simple coin
To toss for life or death.

You are absent where you stay;
Six handles, none
Upon the satin door.

Your heart is locked
For travel. Wind rocks
The trees; I call for you.

II

Paper wasps search pitchforks
Held by morning-glories
Grown since you have gone.

A pocket wren nests
In the winter coat
You left behind.

III

Years like wingstrokes
Move forward and are forgotten.
I stop the car in the cemetery.
Waking, my little girl asks,
"Are we home?"

VISITING HER HOUSE

Little remains: broken windows for each death,
Lost pennies, a stairway to the winter sky
And in spring, gray violets and quince.

She used to like church –
How the benediction spilled across the wooden floor
And washed her praying out the door.

I remember the low field where sun exploded
Walls of granite, and wings of monarchs
Panted up and down like mirrored flames.

She ran through fields of sunflowers
With a black collie always at her side.
Low skies churned with bees for hours.

The last day of her life
She looked at yellow tulips in a vase
And listened to Bach's keyboard music

From another room.

THE MONGOLOID AND THE LUNA

He slapped the kitchen window – frightened me;
Lines on his palms every which way
Split lips whispering through the glass
"Come see."

He had a luna moth in his wagon;
Apple-green and lilac wings
New, drugged by daylight
Perfect.

We watched it till street lights came on
And it lyred its way into night.
He sang it forth
His voice low as the moon.

LATE DERECHO

The sky burns leaves
And wind snaps thunder
Like a blanket
Putting dreams in order.

Lightning's fragrance fills sleep.
I count myself.
Angels familiar with the end
Stop fields with snow.

I know, I know
The wasted chase of storms,
Deciduous friendship –
Ugly until the slum –

Where my friend
Raises the dead.
Certain little things I trust
Without hiding my face.

LAST NIGHT

God's hands
Smell of wood smoke and stars –
The black stove above.

Rough as time
Calluses
Catch and scratch our woods.

He gestures – love.
But scars print
The fear of being struck with a hug.

These hands created my soul.

SOLITARY DEFINEMENT

Incunabula
The pages of the fields;
Golden grass and bramble print
Impressed on snow.
A young fox cries
Against the forest's leather strap
And distance says the one word
Missing from God's name.

I think we live here
In these pages.

The clouds must write their words
And we must touch the varied shade.
Nothing matters then but light –
So dark the wound each parting makes.
Soon that Heaven, the other one,
Will fill the empty glasses
Of the trees with sun
And we exactly know our God.

How we long for the sacred in our lives
And then go broken to a broken God.

MY WIFE

My wife's soul is stronger than mine.
She knows the nonsense of the night;
The permanent magnet of the moon,
The cold-rolled steel of the stars.

Across salvation's safe and silver days
She met the Beast.
He tore her dreams apart
And called them sin.

On Heaven's harshest page of winter,
God's other Bible,
She sets a manger
And calls the chasm Christmas.

Beneath the fascination of a star
She asks for love no one deserves
And wipes her tears away
Before anyone can see.

The soul knows little of itself.
We are God's falling down
And His only love.
I love her in this love.

DOCUMENT

I looked through thirty years
Of rooms to find this page –
A place unclaimed by other words
Where I can write

I love you.

Please keep this someplace safe
With the original –
The one we lose and find
So often that the search

Becomes the words.

REVERIE

I

Take seriously
Sunlight of paper
Place against forgetting;
Touch the blue crocus under ice.

Take seriously
Maple flowers, fragile
As a baby's fingerprints.
Scribble your name on the sky.

II

Hold each word
Like a shell against your ear.
Listen for the ocean –
The used, the fossil sound.

Remember, old prayers are best.
They fill hollows such as these
With reverie.
Always write ahead of words.

TRAPPIST

I wear my grave
Clothes every day; monk's cowl
And leather belt. Matins
In the clay-bright church
Fenceless fields, vellum books
Upon stone floors
These I understand.

Where trees fork light
From place to place, I shout
"Spirit! Angel!" Hands and face
Appear like breath in winter air.
While I gather prayers
Caught like shadows on the ground
Wild dogs eat my Bible. Fireflies
Confused to daylight, mark
The woodwhirl where a dancer
Stepping clear of earth might hear
The turtle's song.

But I have just
A pocketful of days.
Galaxies hold time
The way bricks hold warmth.
A pilgrim waits for me
Along the broken wall
A rider heading home.

ABIDE WITH ME

Bats, hungry violins,
Feed staccato
Under God's crazy mime
Curling gold around the moon.

The white tongue of a sunflower seed
Stops an arrowhead, angry impulse
A hundred years up through the sand,
A cut too slow to feel.

Willows walk around our words
And while we sleep
Clock dust polishes old rings.
If we are safe, we are safe

In a word.

PASSING CONFESSION

Our prayers are Heaven's nectar;
Our lies, the curtains of Hell.

Beware the longings of this earth
Washed up from the sea

This place made holy
This place filigree of ice and sun.

Expect something in the end
But remember

Heaven never begs.

EPITAPH FOR A STRICT LADY

Salvation must have shocked her when she died.
Eyed elaters hit summer windowsills –
Her heart went still, her face no longer lied.
Just fear remained and final whippoorwills.
She missed the cornered glory of her life –
The stone-gray trout, the mink, the adders-tongue.
Old Pan was just a sinner with a fife.
In guilt's sharp tangle all her hope was hung,
A fruit with bitter seeds. The church's floor,
The silver cross – she tried to understand.
The Lover loved somehow inside these doors.
She dared not touch the Shepherd's broken hand.

Hold moss against this anguished heart of Ann.
My Heaven teach her laughter, if it can.

AFTERWORD

Find a place on the ground
To put the sky.
A pond might do
Or a field, November white.

Say of this place
I own everything
From here to Heaven
And back again.

Then sleep, for sleep regards
Our little road to God.

STORMY COMMUNION

I

Frozen by Medusa's tears
November's last chrysanthemum
Blossoms closed.

In a field of marble wings
Tarnished petals turn
Like points of a key –

Revelation small enough to hold.
God puts storms where He wants.

II

You enter this church alone,
Black earrings above calla lilies,
To outlive Hell.

Here, bells break holy bread;
Here, steeples pour new wine.
You have come to say

Let it be real –
Messiah's love affair with time.

MILL

I have no doubt; tomorrow forgiven
Trembles tall as hibiscus –
One flower out of reach
Red as God's clown nose.

And days gone by
Rest gently as moss;
Earth's barrenness undeserved.
Stars say much to the smallest.

A good memory to take to Heaven:
The cinnamon smoke of steel being drilled;
The right sound of spindle speed;
Each axis moved from zero.

Though days like children break our hearts
The song makes sense
If only far away
And heard just once.

EMILY DICKINSON

Yes, I cried
At the slam of woodgrain
Complex as questions –
Love shut.

Young girls see God.
Young girls hear God.

Lost in time, I did dishes
While sunlight honed
The porcelain edge
Of May's last frost.

I hope you do not mind:
I left things where I found them;

Hidden in plain sight.

BLACKBERRIES

A white moth rolls through the grass.
We stop time and rest,
Hands stained and cut,
Picking blackberries in the rain.

With the ear of every flower
We listen. Blue heron,
Thin as fern,
Stalks the face-down pond.

Silence is what we need.
Wrens shake their tails
Against the rising of the firewood moon.
Mites move words from sand.

Forsaken, we walk home.
Messiah for the forgotten
Names this place
World without end.

DO NOT BE AFRAID

We need someone to tell us again that all of us are afraid. Christ is not for the fearless but for those who must hear Him say: "Do not be afraid."

> Padovano

UTERINUS

ANNUNCIATION

Under wings of light
Mary kisses the angel's voice
And her womb fills with a word.

BIRTH

She frames the star
With her fingers –
The star
Bright with God's tears.

LIFE

He says
Do not touch my cloak;
Touch my skin.

DEATH

Under the black rail
His tears
Are tears of an infant
Crying in the womb of creation.

MARY

Mary remembered her angel
When Joseph touched her.
Her moods formed
The Holy Spirit's dream.

Her fear of crossing
The painful desert
Carried Messiah home.
Her sickness gave God flesh.

With the wisemen
She prayed to her son
Sanctifying Eve
In the heart of the church.

STRAW

Though deep the wound as bright the star
We find ourselves in Bethlehem
Repenting where the sun
At last exceeds the night
And angels make it true.

This little place of straw
Begins a thousand songs of joy.
A frightened girl awakens God,
And Eden's Ghost,
The burning forth of Heaven's time,

Can only name His many names
Against the silence of our dreams.

JESUS AND THE PROSTITUTE

They gathered stones
To kill her
From the dust.

His voice stopped them
And His arm
Hooked hers

As though to dance
Heaven's first dance –
Crossover, alone, together.

She loved His tears;
Power
Over death.

Cicadas zippered
The town's small fields;
Heaven kissed her hand.

PETER

I

Jesus laughed when I said
Any wine satisfies
A fisherman's thirst
And plain bread
Is food enough.

The sea went calm against His thoughts.
He kissed me and said
I had told Him
Something wonderful.

II

He cupped sunrise
In His hands and smiled
An old man's smile –
His hair suddenly gray
In slanted light.

And all He said –
It is good.

III

Plainly I told Him,
Time measures baskets
And opens nets to dry;
Time is for old dancers
Under young doves.

But He knew time differently;
His hands, white from prayer,
Gave to mine
Midsummer's double rose.

IV

Pulling me from the Sea of Galilee
His anger baptized my little faith.
His power stung my hands.
And somehow I knew
The pretty part of God's death

Was mine – choice
Before I go against the ground.

V

He frightened me when He left His grave –
As though Heaven took hold of earth
And shook it. But He forgave me.
I ate fish with God.
His scarred hands caught the curl

Of candle fire, and I, His church,
Learned what word to say
Before all else:
Forgiven.

VI

Confusion confirmed Pentecost.
Haggard and holy His words released worlds
And healed beggars in filthy robes.
I spoke of seven loaves of bread
And a few fish

And kissed the root of His cross
Where sprouted Eden's vine.

VII

Death's hurt opens Love;
Shameful law all else.
A humble fisherman, I stand
On fear's last sea
To hold all souls who walk

Toward my gate, circle of Light,
Rebirth of ocean and of land,
Messiah's world
Where blooms midsummer's double rose.

LAZARUS

Jesus preferred the wilderness
But always returned
In time to raise the dead.
The trembling of a little town
Called Him back.

His anger
Shouted to the folded grave,
"Lazarus! Come forth!"

The priest's golden bell would not ring
For chains of miracle bound time.
Even the ocean dared not move.

Lazarus touched the face of Jesus
But could not speak;
He saw the One
Who welcomed him to Paradise.

LAW

God paralyzes God –
Arrests every father's son
Murders every mother's daughter.

Leviticus kills a final time.
The farthest desert owns the golden ark
And music lulls the beast of Paradise.

Angels kiss the lawless grave
While lilies wrap themselves
In needed miracle.

JOSEPH OF ARIMATHEA

I grieve His death
To know Him.
My bones burn like candles
Above His sleep –
Arrested from Paradise.

He hugged lepers
And wept for their healing.
He broke paradigm with parable
And ruined demons
With the laughter of His prayer.

I grieve the Word
To find my voice.
His tomb, earth's throat,
Shouts Easter
And angels wash His feet.

At last an answer
From the room of death:
Eden never fell.

EASTER

White clematis opens like a map.
Familiar angels move the stone
And Eden's gardener
Reclaims the hunted, the divine.

Tabernacle gold
Burns in the streets
Kindling tongues of fire.
A word astounds the earth again.

GIFT

Little One, Veiled Eden,
One star and vespers given –
Vinegar and water, your hidden gift;
Every hope from this, at last.

FOR LOVE IS STRONG AS DEATH
Song of Solomon 8:6

When the stranger (an old friend)
Touches you as though flesh were a window
You will no longer fear the mystery of leaving.

Like coins from a pocket
The tolling of bells
Their portent and silver and time
Will fall from mind at last.

Though friends weep with eyes of broken stone
Laughter will be your hymn
So sure the penetration of last healing.

Death is far to go without a name
The passive pilgrimage
Primitive and promised
Leading to everything meant by love.

HOLY SPIRIT

I have seen you
In the faces of dolls
Old folks caress.
You are the moth under the mirror.

You make sacred
The great stir of fantasy
The gilt edges of books
The Christmas tree in the cemetery.

You took Jesus
Down from His cross.
You hide where we hide
Under the spine of stars.

ANGELS

Messiah sends no angels;
He hides them
In our flesh.

Angels run from the sky
And rarely skate
The shine of lakes.

They shun blue spruce
Even under winter ice.
They sing where the deaf can hear.

Angels are shared.
They drape themselves
Over common hurt.

Angels are shared.
Ask violets and old lovers.
Ask the magic laughter of the grave.

Do not look far away.
His broken wrists
Embrace every wish.

And you will see angels.

TO MISSING PERSONS

I run to Jesus
Crying;
He runs to me
Crying.

His voice remembers every name
Across the rose and sedum of Hell.

Torn to light, He gives
More love
Than anyone
Can see at once.

Mary runs to the hungry gardener
And says, "It is empty! Empty!"

Death is someone's will.

PUNISH NOT MY REST

O carry me, sweet Jesus, where you are.
Your wounds, like kisses, offer peace. I feel
The gentle pulling of your magic star
Past death's white veils and bones, the numb unreal,
The gypsy angel and the biting worms
That silence Heaven's strange invention, mind,
And nurse against all lovely fallen forms.
O punish not my rest but let me find
Earth's little happiness reborn, divine,
And God, a caring force, informal, clear.
There I will walk where walls of roses shine
And scarlet oak replaces every fear.

O carry me, sweet Jesus, where you are;
My soul's compassion on itself unbar.

ANOTHER SKY

Now hush the thunder and the thrush. These hills
Of Bur Oak, tatter-shawled in brown, hold more
Than several seasons and our deaths. Our wills
As pale as dreams caught in the night will pour
Into our Savior's heart, when like a gate,
The wind swings open to another sky –
The sunshine of rebirth where angels wait.
And we will enter there and never die.
Our Bibles carried light as doves; the green
November truth of winter wheat; the scent
Of resurrection plowed from fields: these mean
Our days will end without an argument.

This whirling fermentation, pentecost,
Remembers ecstacy cannot be lost.

WANDERER'S MEDITATION

Evening carries the redbird's song
Hurt from the sky
A promise unfinished.

A cat from Egypt
Cries through the screens –
Eyes green as vineyards
Rounding veraison.

Miracles meander
One heart at a time
And important stars
Can be lost in a tear.

I need Light to write
And an Absolute Redeemer
Dreaming Heaven from a cradle.

For once
The ragged man was right;
Oblivion obeyed. So now

With everyone else
I stagger to salvation
Following the One
Who fell the hardest.

SAINT JOSEPH'S ACADEMY

Brides of Christ follow
Wild geese shaping
The day's number
Across crossfire sunshine.

Octave oaks shade Jesus' stone hands.

And when the moon presses
White as a knuckle
Against their windows
Brides of Christ sing

All others, anonymous their love.

OCTOBER 13, 1917

Three children stop Fatima's storm
And Mary makes the sun to dance.
Across the crowd some faces shine
While others shadowed stay –
Their eyes still looking for the sun.

We taste the sweetness of the sky
And wonder, poor Fatima,
Who will ever say the simple truth –
The kind and settled God of miracle
Who lights this field with ancient mirth?

THE REVEREND TIMOTHY BROWN

He wondered – small funeral –
What to say

Across her gown
Words for a few friends
Waiting where sand
Caught her carriage
Ebony and brass;
What to say
Against the lightning of roots
The thunder of forgotten stones.

He held eternity's clock
The cross of Christ
Above her satin pillow
Frayed ribbons of love.
He could not speak
Until the pews filled with angels
And she danced
She danced

She danced with God
Across his words.

FATHER, FORGIVE THEM

Given enough time
I think we should run away from home.

We will learn the writings of the moss
The intuitions of the storm
The dreams of the stopping grass.

We will forgive earth's rubbed book
The strip-tease words of poetry
The broken champagne of the sea.

Earth frozen, peeled back like white birch,
Will give foothold to pilgrims
Searching for God's last friend.

And just by running away from home
We will, at last, know what we do.

CATCH THE WINDS

And now I know that we must lift the sail
And catch the winds of destiny
Wherever they drive the boat.
To put meaning in one's life may end in madness,
But life without meaning is the torture
Of restlessness and vague desire –
It is a boat longing for the sea and yet afraid.

                Edgar Lee Masters, "George Gray"

TED BANTA

In the rain no one heard
Our fire bucked
Like a pony in quicksand.

The river's noise,
A workman carrying too many tools,
Dominated the small woods.

He said, "It's all a matter of style
And of vanity, and, at best,
Earth is a lonely place to meet God."

By noon the sky cleared.
A sign, "PUBLIC ACCESS,"
Turned away from the wind.

Like women pulling black gowns
Down from around their shoulders
Slender trees laid their shadows on the ground.

"Just by trying," I said,
"We sometimes succeed."
He walked away laughing,

His hands red with wild strawberries.
"I race storms home
Every night."

MANNY SANDOVAL

Manny plays accordion on the beach.
His gypsy mustache curls
And he roars and laughs and laughs.
He dances with sunlight
And plays cards with the rain.
Across dark sand children come –
Magic fingers hold candle fire.

Polkas and children and nicknames of days.

WATCHING LESLIE ANNE'S BIRTH

Across iron bars
I hold my wife's hands
As though they are important wishes.

At last a nurse motions me out.
I put on a surgical gown –
The mask upside down across my beard.

Just as the sun's top
Pushes through the leaves
Of another October Sunday

I see a cut, water, then the faded head,
Her first cry at first light.
The nurse washes the baby's eyes.

As I hold her and look
Towards the Halloween black trees
And chill around the large sun

I think something for her:
Long life lines, deep and clear,
And galaxies bright with genesis.

C - The Place In The Woods/Read, America! 1996
Reprinted with permission

TO R. ABOUT BEETLES

She is most delicate
This friend
Blossoming shyly beyond girlhood
Her thoughts as silent as long hair
Her hopes as clear and scattered
As the winter stars.

I remember watching her hesitate
On the shadowed porch
As though she feared the weight
Of April wind
Expanding evenly
Over gray and yellow lawns.

Later we opened
Winter-blackened leaves
Beneath path stones.
Green and purple shells
Flashed to life, awakened
By the warmth.

With eyes half shut
She smiled at the sky
And placed the stone
Back on the mystery;
Lives, unharmed by frost,
Though frail as fantasy.

C - The Place In The Woods/Read, America! 1996
Reprinted with permission

GREEN THE LILAC WOOD

Wood cut; cord evened:
Her sister died,
The evil one,

The one
She would not grieve.
No words needed.

Tears
Come from a place
Deeper than evil.

AND END

Her father died downstairs.
She cried in an old Dutch room,
Six walls, none square.

A child of common vows
She suffered greatly
And asked little.

The preacher drove her door to door
To say God's truth: we are never
Separated, and it is good to cry.

She wondered about the winter clouds
Cataloging days, and the moon –
A slice of apple over hickory woods.

SANDY

Like black leeches, tumors
Curl around my lungs. I must leave
My children, my dear children
Before they grow. They cry
Softly in the night. With old pain
Killer, they inject their dolls.

Death is just a box to keep
Things in. Crows carry
The key in their laughter.
Through frozen mornings,
Redemption's rough patina,
I run away

With myself.

EARLY SNOW

I

Calliope music, please,
For leaves and children
Under wide chalk streak skies.

Halloween's old world wind
Burns woods to the ground –
Sweet, invisible smoke.

Thistle pods paw the barn
Window. Winter hides
Like a ghost behind the door.

II

Snow at night
Far and slow –
Rehearsal for an early eternity.

Carved pumpkins collapse around candles.
Everyone sleeps
In the old photo found again.

Tomorrow we will look for the sun
And find a brass key
Dropped in cold water.

FENN VALLEY VINEYARDS

I

Stainless steel and ice –
Will it ever be Spring?
Snow spatters underground towers
Where wines settle, cold-stable.

Trailing angles of geese signal
Above vineyards sloping
Towards Todd Farm.
The peaceful cut of pruners
Names next year's wines:
Riesling, Chancellor, Chardonnay, Seyval.

Heavy alpha snow blurs square vineyards
Into circles. The sleep of vines
Enters pruners' arms, minds – hypnotic,
Distant, rhythmic. Smoke
From farmhouse chimneys spices
Far-field conversations.

Walter checks trellis anchors;
He tightens wires under December evenings
Dimming pink to black.
Maintenance season splits his hands.

II

Millions of dollars spent to see
Shatter –
The small lacy spice
Of grape blossoms.

Hutchin's Lake reflects
White and pink orchards.
Storms, frost, sunshine, pollination
Dominate our days.

Small clusters
Swell
Form shoulders,
Color.

Hand over hand
New shoots fill summer trellises.
Wires stretch
Waiting for autumn pickers.

III

Crush,
Season of hornets and long hours,
Brings grapes in endless tons.
Crushers and presses shake
Concrete floors. We send

Time
Through the centrifuge
A whole year at once,
The vintage
Purified.

Fermentations build and ebb like storms.
The winemaker's luck
Controls
New wines accurately as trees
Space leaves on random branches.

We work late at night,
Dripping wet, crazy-like.
Sometimes anger asks
Why make wine? We work
Kindly or cruelly

With or without an answer.

SELAH

Time does not move forward;
Eden's gleaning pulls it back.
Chasing after after, clocks,
Like mirrors, turn time around.

Our births look the wrong direction.
Tomorrow is the cinder of today.
Our maps grow edges.
Our galaxies tarnish into days.

Time does not push like the wind;
It pulls our breath back into us
Gathering a word strong beyond belief –
A word against the night we hurry to.

We hear the silence of its saying
Standing asleep in the earth,
And time laughs
Like a child under a table.

SAINT TERESA OF AVILA

Teresa walks barefoot through the Renaissance.
She wonders, "Will there be pentecost
For the poor in spirit, for the lost?"

Under lakes
Snails trace exact
Courses of stars.

SHALL WE DISCUSS I LOVE YOU

I

Flesh is poor shelter for my soul;
Death's time change cuts near my heart.
Will I forget the sun and moon entirely
Or release rain from memory, bright windows,
Frost ancient as zero? Will place alone prevail—
Dandelions turning white
A brass bucket of fish heads
Someone hammering in the cold garage?

I fear the small voices who point to Bethlehem
And the star fallen from Satan's hand;
History becomes hammer and nails.
Earth cries like an old man
But the sky is full of talk.
Your wasted face come clear upon the cross,
Thorns gathered from the time time's contract ends –
To these my nod of faith, consent to miracle.

Salvation is all scar.

II

Jesus, this reputation received by asking
Does it say I am not one of my kind?
Or is my live nickel and dime love
Common along the narrow way
This hand-me-down earth?

You know me alive and dead; tell me
Will my dreams clear of falling days
And find your new creation
Sweet as fresh-hewn wood?

Will angels put the centuries away
Like old riding coats –
Their hands gestures of fire
Above time's coarse cloth?

Forgive me. I am lost
Between staying and going.
I kneel and the Big Dipper hits the road.

UNDER THE TREMENDOUS OAK

Some days faith tips in my head
Like a flat stone
And prayers herd angels
Like black cows out of books.
I prefer to feel
We are right in some ways.

Some say Heaven begins beyond
Fields of wind-run flowers
Where bumblebees roll
Like lions in the yellow dust.
Guessing, we sense seasons never seen
And the fox sleeps in the filaree.

We are right in some ways.
The virgin, the mystic, the prostitute
Touched the violence, touched
The most beautiful man on earth.
All anger passed through Him and became love:
This is the only dream come true.

Each of us was given a light through the darkness –
The murderer in his forty-winter house,
Ballerinas dancing on wet grass –
Gods of silver
Gods of gold:
These are right in some ways.

I will live a peasant
Under the tremendous oak.
Roosters will chase the Model T,
And children in the pumpkin woods
Will sing songs left from severe years. Father
Will push his wheelbarrow past the stormy barn.

We are right in some ways;
The most beautiful man said so.
Salvation lives hidden ahead of us.
We turn pages in our books
And only begin to love Him,
So much light thrown in our faces.

His love for us grows wildly
On trellises of stars.

SING OF THIS

We have no place to go
But to Heaven.

He told me this
Whose voice raised the dead.
Do you remember the star

Frightened shepherds followed
To Bethlehem? It leads you now
Into these words;

Words with no place to go
But into your heart,
For your heart knows

The way to Heaven.
Children sing of this on Christmas.

PROPHET

Under the slow protest sign of the moon
He lives alone.
Hurrying through the Porcupine Mountains,
He scuffs freezing rain
Along ledges holding Lake Superior.
Only weakest branches sing in the wind.

He never changes the subject
In the middle of a storm.
Hidden books of angels
And opened ones of rage
Say, Believe in nothing;
Nothing will be real.

He admits we need someone
Against our doubt –
Someone to figure Heaven in.
And the one we need is here.
Pages invisible between pages
Tell before the rocks cry out.

MORE THAN EVER

Fireflies attend the deep well of the grape
And the moon lifts water from the fields.

Why would God forget us?
His robe is the color of our souls.

He comes to us, a perfect flower cut,
The tortured purchase of final years.

Kicked-over tombstones,
The stars, list our names.

The living cannot see night
And the dead cannot see fire.

The gold of pardon in our hands,
Bartered home we go,

A place at last to sing –
Scriptures of timbrels and tines.

BLUEBIRD COOPS

He placed them carefully
On posts, just this high;
Cedar boxes clean enough for nests.

"Bluebirds search this time of year
Out of sight in clearing February sky
For lonely, open places."

The woods are still
The same dark harpsichord.
No one remembered when he died

To take his mailbox down.
But I have memorized that sky
Where bluebirds look

And I believe with him
They will return:
A whispered song takes back the earth.

BEECH TREES

They abhor touch;
Even shadows crossed
Send branches crookedly away.

Yet, blind to the sky,
Roots congregate
Holding the forest up.

Carvings on trunks
Show lovers' hearts
And blueprints of the wind.

Hollows gather fallen leaves
The color of oiled chain
Just begun to rust.

Bill Timmer

Del Sneller was born in Holland, Michigan in 1945. He studied at Hope College and Michigan State University, where in 1972 he received his doctorate in literature. He has been a college professor, a rare book collector, a factory worker, a farm hand, and the cellar master of a large winery. For the last twelve years he has been a salesman for All-Phase Electric Supply Company.

Del and his wife still live in Holland. In their spare time they farm their vineyard of wine grapes. They have three daughters and three granddaughters.

In 1976 Stone Country Press published Del's first book, *Secret and Silent in the Earth*. He has read his poetry for many high school, college, and church groups.